Give Them the Bayonet!

A GUIDE TO THE BATTLE FOR HENRY HILL

JULY 21, 1861

A walking tour

By

JoAnna M. McDonald

BURD STREET PRESS

Copyright © 1999 by JoAnna M. McDonald

This Burd Street Press publication
was printed by
Beidel Printing House, Inc.
63 West Burd Street
Shippensburg, PA 17257-0152 USA

In respect for the scholarship contained herein, the acid-free paper used in this book meets the guidelines for permanence and durability of the Committee on Production Guidelines for Book Longevity of the Council on Library Resources.

For a complete list of available publications
please write
Burd Street Press
Division of White Mane Publishing Company, Inc.
P.O. Box 152
Shippensburg, PA 17257-0152 USA

Library of Congress Cataloging-in-Publication Data

McDonald, JoAnna M., 1970-
    Give them the bayonet! : a guide to the battle for Henry Hill,
July 21, 1861 : a walking tour / by JoAnna M. McDonald.
        p.   cm.
    Includes bibliographical references and index.
    ISBN 1-57249-107-8 (alk. paper)
    1. Bull Run, 1st Battle of, Va., 1861. 2. Manassas National
Battlefield Park (Va.)--Tours.   I. Title.
E472.18.M37   1999
973.7'31--dc21   98-56449
                                                                  CIP

PRINTED IN THE UNITED STATES OF AMERICA

To my sisters,
Elizabeth and Rebecca,
and
To the residents of Manassas

Contents

Acknowledgments

I would like to first thank my parents, family and friends for supporting me through this research and writing process. Two of the most influential historians in this project were Jim Burgess, Museum Director at the Manassas Battlefield Park, and John Hennessy, noted Civil War author. Jim provided excellent constructive criticism throughout my rewriting stage, and provided several photos from the Manassas archives. In addition, he took me on a guided tour of the area. John, as well, contributed some very helpful literary advice.

The Military History Institute's staff at the Carlisle Barracks, Carlisle, Pennsylvania again showed great cooperation.

Introduction

On Sunday, July 21, 1861, at 6:00 a.m., the First Battle of Manassas (Bull Run) began. Brigadier General Irvin McDowell commanded the Union army, Army of Northeastern Virginia (35,732).[1] Two Confederate armies united near Manassas Junction, Virginia. Brigadier General Pierre G.T. Beauregard led his Army of the Potomac, and General Joseph E. Johnston controlled the Army of the Shenandoah. Their combined strength totalled nearly 30,000.[2]

For about three hours the fighting focused around the Stone Bridge on the Warrenton Pike. The action then shifted to Matthews Hill. From 10:00 a.m. to 11:30 a.m. the battle raged. Two Union brigades, however, outnumbered the Confederates, and they retreated to Henry Hill.

The battle for Henry Hill has long been forgotten by many Civil War students. Yet, it was a very traumatic and trying time for those soldiers who experienced their baptism by fire. Since this was their first fight it is a very difficult battle to piece together.

From 1:30–4:00 p.m. chaos reigned on Henry Hill. For purposes of explication, the complex, continuous action has been divided into fifteen stages; after the second stage it is impossible to provide an accurate time. There are several reasons for the confusing nature of this contest: 1) Fifteen Union regiments and thirteen Confederate regiments charged and counterattacked so quickly that the action became a whirlpool of obscurity. 2) Afterwards, not even the participants could provide a clear account. 3) Many Union regiments fired only a few rounds before falling back; as another regiment replaced them, the retreating and charging men became intermingled. 4) As a result, several Union regiments became so disorganized that the soldiers fought in smaller, makeshift battalions. 5) Confederate units combined as well. Those that assailed Matthews Hill either joined with other regiments, battled in makeshift battalions, or rested behind the lines.

To add to the confusion, many Union regiments wore gray uniforms which created a distressing dilemma for Confederate and Union alike. The similarity of flags also contributed to officers mistaking enemy regiments for their own. Frequently one could hear, "Stop firing; you are shooting at your friends."

Five stops are provided for the visitor (see map 1). The visitor who wishes to remain in one general area should remain near the Henry House and Ricketts' battery. Note: The text's stops do not coincide with the National Park's numbering.

—MAP 1—
MODERN MAP

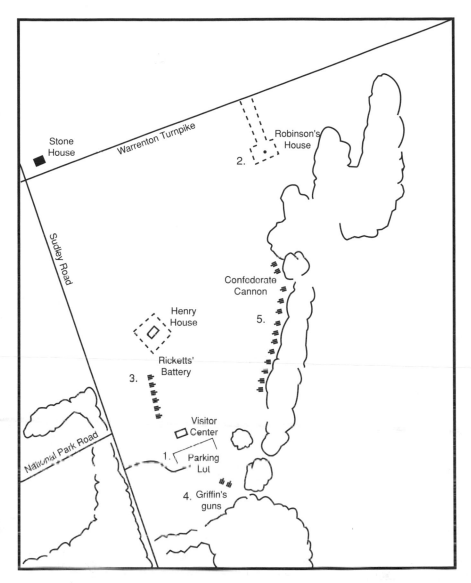

Stone House

Warrenton Turnpike

Robinson's House

2.

Sudley Road

Confederate Cannon

Henry House

5.

Ricketts' Battery

3.

National Park Road

Visitor Center

1. Parking Lot

4. Griffin's guns

Stop 1: National Park Visitor Center; Stop 2: Robinson's House; Stop 3: Henry House/ Ricketts' Battery; Stop 4: Griffin's Two Howitzers; Stop 5: Confederate Cannon

Lull in the Infantry Fight.

CONFEDERATE · (12:00–1:00 P.M.)

"I'll support your battery."

—*Brigadier General Thomas Jackson*

Captain John Imboden
(Seen here in a general's uniform)

Brigadier General
Thomas Jackson
(Seen here in his lieutenant general's
uniform)

The Confederates used the respite to reinforce Henry Hill. Brigadier General Thomas Jackson's Virginia brigade reached the area first about 12:00 noon. Riding at the head of his men, Jackson met Captain Imboden as he was retreating. Enraged at being left alone on the hill, Imboden, swearing, vented his frustration to Jackson. The general, however, calmly replied, "I'll support your battery. Unlimber right here."[1] Imboden unlimbered his three cannon about three-hundred yards from the Henry House on the southeastern edge of the hill. Shortly after this thirteen additional cannon arrived, previously ordered up by Johnston and Beauregard. Immediately, Jackson deployed them near Imboden's guns. Captain Imboden then limbered his cannon and went to the rear to refill his ammunition caissons while the newly arrived cannoneers continued to duel with the Union artillerymen.

After speaking with Imboden, Brigadier General Bee rode up and shouted to Jackson, "General, they are beating us back!"

Jackson replied, "Then, sir, we will give them the bayonet..."[2]

Determined to stay and fight, Jackson ordered his men to lie down behind the cannon and await reinforcements. Many of the Union artillery shells overshot the cannon and exploded near the Virginia infantry, terrifying the raw recruits. Despite the shelling, by choosing the reverse slope of Henry Hill, Jackson displayed brilliant tactical insight. Two houses stood on Henry Hill (actually a plateau): Mrs. Judith Henry's house overlooked Young's Branch and the Sudley Road-Warrenton Turnpike Intersection. About six-hundred yards northeast of her house, Mr. James Robinson, a freedman, lived in a small farmhouse. A thick wooded area lined the southern edge of the plateau.[3] Realizing his brigade was outnumbered (2,412),[4] Jackson hid his force in the pine thicket below the crest of the hill (see map 2). Had he placed his brigade at the crest of Henry Hill they would have been subject to direct artillery and infantry fire, and their strength quickly discovered. Consequently, the Union might have pressed their attack. As it was, the reverse slope position concealed Jackson's brigade and gave the Virginians protection from enemy fire. If the Union infantry crested the hill, they still had to cross three-hundred yards in an open field before engaging the enemy within the trees, thus allowing the Confederate artillery and infantry time to cut down any small unit attacks.[5]

Shortly after Jackson deployed his men, Johnston and Beauregard arrived at Henry Hill (about 12:00 noon). The generals decided to split their responsibilities: Beauregard took immediate command of the troops on the hill, and Johnston assumed control over the entire line, directing

—MAP 2—
LULL IN THE INFANTRY BATTLE · HENRY HILL
12:30–1:30 P.M.
STOP 1

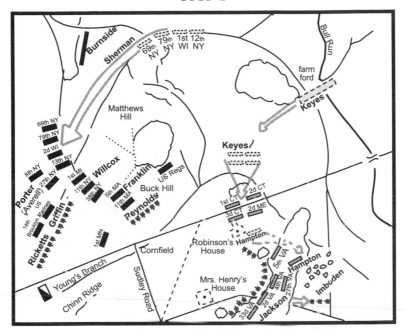

Sherman's brigade deploys near Porter's troops while Keyes begins his assault near the Robinson House. McDowell assembles about 18,860 men while Confederate Brigadier General Jackson's brigade (2,412) awaits another Union assault. Thirteen Confederate cannon continue to duel with the Union batteries. Captain Imboden takes his three cannon to restock the ammunition chests.

the rest of the reinforcements—Holmes', Bonham's, Elzey's, and Early's brigades—to Henry Hill.

Beauregard, in the meantime, rode up and down the field trying to rally the disorganized squads from Evans', Bee's and Bartow's regiments. Shells exploded around him; one disemboweled his horse. He fell hard but showed no sign of distress and quickly mounted another horse.[6] By 1:30 p.m. Beauregard calculated he had 6,500 men and thirteen pieces of artillery at his command.[7] (Beauregard seems to have considered the casualties already suffered in Evans', Bee's and Bartow's regiments when he calculated this number. In actuality, Beauregard had only Jackson's and Hampton's units ready [3,012 men]. Evans', Bee's and Bartow's units were still disorganized and had suffered heavy casualties. Reinforcements, however, rapidly marched to their aid.)

UNION

"They are running! The day is ours."

—Brigadier General Irvin McDowell

While the Confederates hurriedly established a battle line, more Union brigades reached Matthews Hill. Earlier, around 10:30 a.m., McDowell had directed Tyler to "press the attack" at Stone Bridge.[8] Tyler, however, did not relay the order to his brigade commanders until after 11:00 a.m. When the directive arrived, Colonel Sherman immediately crossed Bull Run at a small farm ford.[9] In his memoirs Sherman described the situation:

> *We found no difficulty in crossing over, and met with no opposition in ascending the steep bluff opposite with our infantry, but it was impassable to the artillery, and I sent word back to Captain Ayres to follow if possible, otherwise to use his discretion...Advancing slowly and cautiously with the head of the column, to give time for the regiments in succession to close up their ranks, we first encountered a party of the enemy* [possibly stragglers from the 4th South Carolina or Georgia troops] *retreating along a cluster of pines; Lieutenant-Colonel Haggerty, of the Sixty-ninth, without orders, rode out alone, and endeavored to intercept their retreat. One of the enemy, in full view, at short range, shot Haggerty, and he fell dead from his horse.*[10]

After a short fire fight the Confederates retreated, and Sherman's brigade continued to Matthews Hill, forming behind Porter's regiments.

In the meantime, McDowell and his staff rode through the Union troops shouting, "Victory! Victory! The day is ours! They are running! They are in retreat"[11] For the moment 6,500 Confederates stood between McDowell and the Confederate rear; however, only 3,000 were battle-ready. McDowell had between 13,000–18,000 men and twenty-four cannon on hand. If he acted quickly and continued the assault he could get behind the Confederate army and completely rout the remaining brigades (see map 2). Though the soldiers awaited the order to pursue, McDowell did not press the advantage. He assumed the Confederates were completely demoralized, and his victory could be taken at any time, a conjecture which would cost him the day.[12]

Go to Stop 2: Robinson's House

Robinson's House

(The Robinson House was destroyed by an arsonist in 1993.)

FIRST STAGE
ROBINSON HOUSE · (1:30 P.M.–2:00 P.M.)

"...the fire became so hot...it...
would have annihilated my whole line."

—*Colonel Erasmus Keyes*

Opposing Regiments

CONFEDERATE:	UNION:
5th Virginia	2d Maine
380	772
Hampton's Legion	3d Connecticut
600	789

In this fight approximately 980 Confederates battled 1,552 Union troops.

After Sherman's brigade crossed Bull Run, Colonel Erasmus Keyes' brigade followed. Brigadier General Tyler, their division commander, however, ordered Keyes to "take a battery on a height in front."[1] Keyes therefore directed two of his regiments, the 2d Maine and 3d Connecticut, to press the attack on Henry Hill.

Having left their coats and knapsacks on the east side of Bull Run, the New Englanders ran down the slopes and across Young's Branch (½ mile). Exhausted and hot, the men stopped at the Warrenton Turnpike and quickly deployed—the 3d Connecticut on the right and the 2d Maine on the left.[2]

At the center of the Maine line, Color Sergeant William S. Deane unfurled the regimental colors, nicknamed the "California flag." Women from Maine, now living in San Francisco, had made the flag and sent it home to their boys.[3]

Robinson's House, circa 1880

With the flag uncased, Colonel Jameson led the 2d Maine forward. Only advancing one hundred yards, Keyes directed the two regiments to lie down and load their weapons. The New Englanders loaded their smoothbore muskets with .69 caliber buck and ball, and yelling like demons, rushed up the hill. (A Confederate later described the "Yankee" yell as sounding like "Hoo-ray! Hoo-ray! Hoo-ray!" The first sound "hoo," if heard at all, was a short, low, indistinct tone; "Ray," a high, long tone, slightly deflected at the end. Many times it sounded like "heigh-ray!")[4]

Nearly surrounded, Hampton's Legion fell back. The 5th Virginia and 2d Maine, both in gray uniforms, hesitated. The 5th then fired, but without the support of Hampton's Legion, they retreated and redeployed in a small wooded area, about one hundred yards south of the Robinson House. Using the trees as cover, the 5th sent a devastating fire into the Union regiments.[5]

Near the Robinson House, the 2d Maine and 3d Connecticut lay down behind the fence previously occupied by the Confederates. Their old smoothbores became hot and fouled with black powder, but they continued to frantically load and fire. Men swore, mad with rage and zeal; yet, with only a small fence protecting them, the casualties mounted. A bullet passed through Color Sergeant Deane's throat, and he quickly bled to death; Captain Elisha N. Jones fell paralyzed, his spine broken when a bullet drove through his body. He later died from this wound.

—MAP 3—
HENRY HILL · FIRST STAGE
1:30–2:00 P.M.
STOP 2

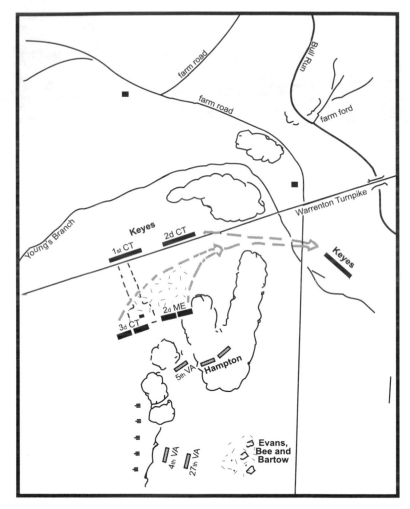

A close-up view of the 3d Connecticut and 2d Maine's attack. Hampton's Legion and the 7th Georgia are forced back, but the 5th Virginia repositions in the pine thicket and sends a devasting fire into the New Englanders. Keyes then retreats and redeploys. His brigade is essentially behind the Confederate line. Yet, out of touch with McDowell, his brigade stands idle throughout the remainder of the battle.

Keyes remembered: "the fire became so hot that an exposure to it of five minutes would have annihilated my whole line";[6] however, instead of supporting the 2d Maine and 3d Connecticut with his other two regiments, Keyes and Tyler ordered the men to fall back to the Warrenton Turnpike. Under Tyler's guidance, Keyes moved his entire brigade by the left flank (see map 3). Due to the confusion, poor communication and generalship, Keyes' attack did not coordinate with McDowell's assault on Henry Hill, and for the remainder of the day Keyes' brigade stood idle, virtually behind the Confederate right flank.

(The 2d Maine lost 37 killed and wounded with 118 missing; the 3d Connecticut suffered 17 killed and wounded, 18 missing.)

Go to Stop 3: Henry House/Ricketts' battery

SECOND STAGE* · (1:45–2:15 P.M.)

"...mark my words, they will not support us."
—Captain Charles Griffin

Union Artillery Officers

Captain James B. Ricketts, age 44
Company I, 1st U.S. Artillery
(6 guns)
(Seen in his brigadier general's uniform)

Captain Charles Griffin, age 36
Company D, 5th U.S. Artillery
(5 guns)

After nearly two hours of resting and reorganizing his forces, McDowell, at 1:30 p.m., told his chief of artillery, Major William F. Barry, to send two batteries to Henry Hill. Barry directed Captain Charles Griffin's and Captain James B. Ricketts' batteries forward. Both captains opposed the new position; the batteries would be in the open and too close to the Confederate infantry. In addition, they needed

---

*The U.S. Marine battalion (250), commanded by Colonel John G. Reynolds, also participated in the initial infantry action. The majority of recruits, however, were rookies and after the first shots they ran for cover.

infantry support to protect their cannon from a Confederate assault. Major Barry assured Griffin that the Fire Zouaves (11th New York) would support the batteries. Skeptical, Griffin retorted, "I will go; but mark my words, they will not support us."[1] Griffin's five guns (one had become jammed earlier and was left on John Dogan's farm) led the way; Ricketts' six followed. The convoy moved through the valley, across Young's Branch, and down the Sudley Road. Due to a misunderstanding in directions, Lieutenant Charles E. Hazlett, on the first cannon, turned right and headed for the Chinn farm. Ricketts' battery, however, turned left into Mrs. Henry's yard, and unlimbered to the right of the house (see map 4). Ricketts recounted, "I had scarcely got into battery before I saw some of my horses fall and some of my men wounded by the sharpshooters [who were hiding in the house]. I turned my guns upon the house and literally riddled it."[2] Unknown to the Union artillerymen, Mrs. Judith Henry lay in her bed.

VIGNETTE:
MRS. JUDITH HENRY

During the mid-day lull, after several shells struck near the Henry House, Ellen and John Henry attempted to carry their elderly mother, Judith, out of her home. Their hope of safety was a farm several miles away. The battle, however, intensified around them, and they returned carrying their mother back to her bedroom. Terrified, the family cowered as the shells fell in and around the house. One shell burst directly in Judith's room, wounding her in the neck and side, and blowing off part of one foot. Her colored servant, a hired girl named Lucy Griffiths, was also wounded in the arm. Judith died later that day from her wounds.

After the battle the Confederates buried Mrs. Henry a few yards from her house. She was eighty-five years old and the only civilian killed during the battle.[3]

While Ricketts' artillery battered the Henry House, Griffin redirected his five cannon to Henry Hill and deployed

—MAP 4—
HENRY HILL · SECOND STAGE
1:45–2:30 P.M.
STOP 3

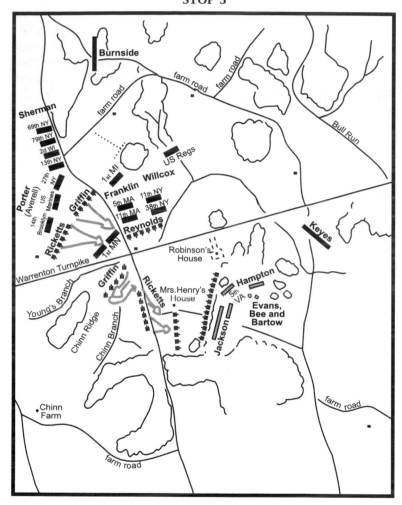

Finally, after two hours, McDowell sends Captain Griffin's and Ricketts' batteries to Henry Hill. Griffin's battery gets sidetracked while Ricketts' battery unlimbers to the right of Mrs. Henry's house.

A drawing by Leon J. Fremaux of Mrs. Judith Henry's house as seen after the battle. Her house became the center of the fighting during the afternoon and was riddled by artillery and musket fire.

them to the left of the house.[4] For over half-an-hour thirteen Confederate cannon (eleven smoothbore and two rifled), and eleven Union cannon (nine rifled and two smoothbore) dueled at less than 300 yards. Lieutenant Hazlett recalled the cannonade:

> *We had been in action there for some time; the fire was exceedingly hot; and being in such close range of the enemy we were losing a great many men and horses. We were in full relief on top of the hill, while they were a little behind the crest of the hill. We presented a better mark for them than they did for us.*[5]

In addition to these complications, the Union rifled cannon, which were more effective at longer ranges, either overshot the Confederate cannon and exploded over Jackson's brigade, or the shells bored several feet into the ground and then exploded, the fragments dispersing harmlessly into the earth.

As the shells burst over the prone Virginians, men prayed, "Oh Lord! Have mercy upon me! Have mercy upon me!" And, nearby, someone cried, "Me too, Lord! Me too, Lord!"[6] To ease the men's fears, Beauregard and Jackson continued to ride up and down the line. Jackson shouted, "Steady, men! steady! all's well!"[7]

While Jackson's brigade hugged the earth, three Union infantry regiments (U.S. Marine battalion, 11th New York, and the 1st Minnesota) arrived and deployed in the rear of Griffin's and Ricketts' guns (see map 5). Two companies from the 1st Minnesota approached to within fifty to sixty yards of the Confederate line.

At first, Colonel Arthur Cummings, 33d Virginia, mistook the line for arriving Confederate reinforcements and yelled, "Cease firing, you are firing on friends!" As Cummings shouted, a volley came from the Union line; Private John Casler of the 33d sarcastically cried, "Friends, hell! That looks like it."[8]

Similar confusion occurred on the Union side. Several Minnesota men fired at the body of troops to their front. Their colonel, William A. Gorman, "Willis," exclaimed, "Stop firing—they are our friends."[9] The Confederates then answered with a volley of their own, and the Union officers ordered their men to lie down and fire. An 11th New York Zouave private recalled his experience:

> ...Crashing through the cornfield, singing and whistling around our ears, making the air blue and sulphurous with smoke, came a storm of bullets upon us from the woods in front. "Down, every one of you," cried the Colonel. And we went down just in time to escape the second volley. No orders came all along the line. One and then another would jump up and fire and then lie down to reload. Some started toward the woods on their own account, crawling slowly along in hopes to get sight of the foe.[10]

One bullet struck Colonel Noah Farnham, 11th New York, in the left side of the head. (He died later in Washington, D.C.)[11]

As smoke covered the battlefield, Sergeant John G. Merritt, with several of his Minnesota comrades, ran toward the Confederate color-bearer.

> The man who carried the colors was about five feet ten or eleven inches, dark complexioned, with black

—MAP 5—
HENRY HOUSE/RICKETTS' BATTERY (STOP 3)
SECOND STAGE, *Continued*
STOP 3

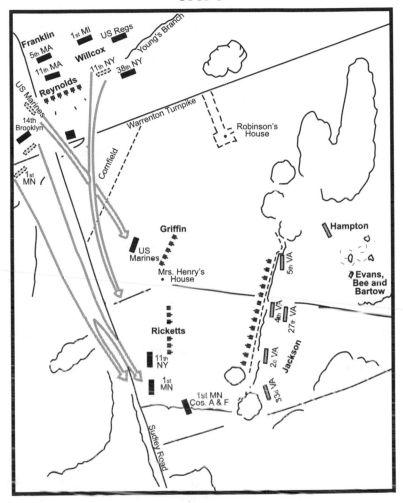

Griffin's battery finally unlimbers to the left of Mrs. Henry's house. The U.S. Marine battalion lies down behind Griffin's battery while the 11th New York and 1st Minnesota come up the hill to Ricketts' right. In the battle confusion two companies from the 1st Minnesota are separated from the regiment.

hair, slight mustache and black eyes; he with oth-
ers about him wore gray clothes and black slouch
hats; some one was trying to form them. The color-
bearer had his coat unbuttoned, with his hat on
the back of his head. As I got within a couple feet
of him I commanded him in a peremptory manner
to surrender, and at the same time Dudley, Durfee
and myself cocked our guns. I grabbed the colors
out of his hand; he and one or two more said, 'Don't
shoot! don't shoot!'...As soon as I grabbed the col-
ors out of the Johnnie's hands I told him to follow
me quick, and at the same time told my men to get
back to the regiment as soon as possible. Dudley,
Grim and myself were laughing at the easy thing
we had [done], and all of us running for the regi-
ment as fast as we could go, when—bang! bang!
bang! came a volley after us, killing Grim and the
comrade whose name I have forgotten, and at the
same time a dozen or more of Rebs ran after us,
some of them hollering 'Kill the d——d black aboli-
tion, red-shirt Yankee,....'[12]

The Confederates fired again, killing Durfee and wounding
Merritt in the leg. He continued to carry the flag, but the angry
Confederates soon overwhelmed him. One man hit Merritt over
the head with the butt of his musket and pulled the flag from
his hands. The entire episode lasted only minutes.

The 11th New York and 1st Minnesota fired four to five
rounds per man and then began to retreat down the hill
and gather on Sudley Road—only fifteen to twenty minutes
had passed.

On the Confederate side Colonel James Ewell Brown
Stuart, commander of the First Virginia Cavalry, saw the
retreating Union troops and mistook them for Confederates.
He rode out amongst them and exclaimed, "Don't run, boys;
we are here." The Union troops ignored him, and Stuart
soon saw a man carrying the U.S. flag. He immediately rode
back to his cavalrymen. Cutting right and left, Stuart's 150
horsemen charged into the Union troops. Virginian Lieutenant William Willis Blackford participated in the charge.

...when within a couple of horses's lengths of them,
I leaned down, with my carbine cocked, thumb on

Private John Casler, age 23
Company A, "Potomac Guards"
33d Virginia
450
(Self-portrait)

Colonel William A. Gorman
1st Minnesota
900
(Seen in his brigadier general's uniform)

Colonel Noah Farnham
11th New York
900
Mortally wounded in the head; he died August 14, 1861.

Sergeant John G. Merritt
1st Minnesota
Later won the Congressional Medal of Honor for attempting to capture a Confederate flag.

*hammer and forefinger on trigger, and fixed my eye
on a tall fellow I saw would be the one my course
would place in the right position for the carbine,
while the man next to him, in front of the horse, I
would have to leave to Comet. I then plunged the
spurs into Comet's flanks and he evidently thought
I wanted him to jump over this strange looking wall
I was riding him at, for he rose to make the leap;
but he was too close and going too fast to rise higher
than the breast of the man, and he struck him full
on the chest, rolling him over and over under his
hoofs and knocking the rear rank man to one side.
As Comet rose to make the leap, I leaned down
from the saddle, rammed the muzzle of the carbine into the stomach of my man and pulled the
trigger. I could not help feeling a little sorry for the
fellow as he lifted his handsome face to mine while
he tried to get his bayonet up to meet me; but he
was too slow, for the carbine blew a hole as big as
my arm clear through him.*[13]

Two companies of Zouaves rushed the cavalrymen with
bayonets and attempted to stab their opponents. Other
Union infantry scattered throughout the woods and down
Sudley Road. Thinking they had routed the regiments, the
Confederate cavalrymen rode back to the Confederate line
(see map 6).

Sudley Road, looking north, toward the Stone House, circa 1880

—MAP 6—
HENRY HOUSE/RICKETTS' BATTERY
SECOND STAGE, *Continued*
STOP 3

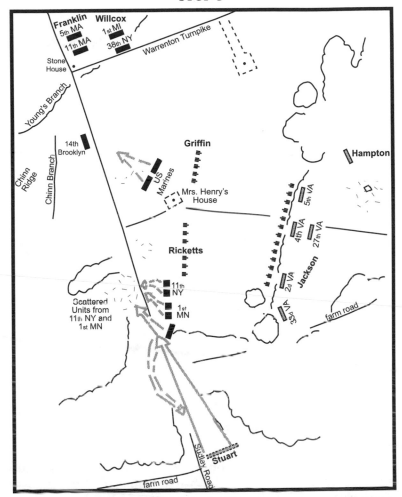

Confederate and Union regiments exchange musket fire; the U.S. Marines break immediately. The 11th New York and 1st Minnesota fire four or five rounds per man and retreat to Sudley Road. Confederate Colonel Jeb Stuart's Virginia cavalrymen charge into the disorganized troops. After a short melée the Virginians break off their attack.

Go to Stop 4: Griffin's two howitzers, near the visitor's center parking lot (see map 1, page ix)

THIRD STAGE

"Charge bayonets!"

—*Colonel Arthur Cummings, 33d Virginia*

Opposing Regiments

CONFEDERATE:	UNION:
33d Virginia	Company D, 5th U.S. Artillery
450	2 guns

A few minutes after the encounter with the cavalry, groups of soldiers from the 11th New York and 1st Minnesota gathered behind Ricketts' and Griffin's cannon. Other New Yorkers soon arrived as well. The 38th New York lay down directly behind Griffin's three guns near the Henry House. At the same time, Griffin redeployed two guns to Ricketts' far right (see map 7). He planned to move them to a less exposed position and send an enfilading fire down through the Confederate line of artillery pieces. Unlimbering, the artillerymen readied their cannon with shell.

Griffin saw a body of infantrymen forming to his front and ordered the cannon to be loaded with canister. Major Barry, Griffin's commander, rode up and said, "Captain, don't fire there; those are your battery support."

Griffin replied, "They are Confederates; as certain as the world, they are Confederates."

Barry answered, "I know they are your battery support." Obeying his commander, the Union artillerymen hesitated. The regiment, however, was the 33d Virginia.

Coming within forty yards of the cannon, they let loose a deadly volley and charged.[1] Private Casler, 33d Virginia, recalled the assault:

20

—MAP 7—
GRIFFIN'S TWO HOWITZERS
THIRD STAGE
STOP 4

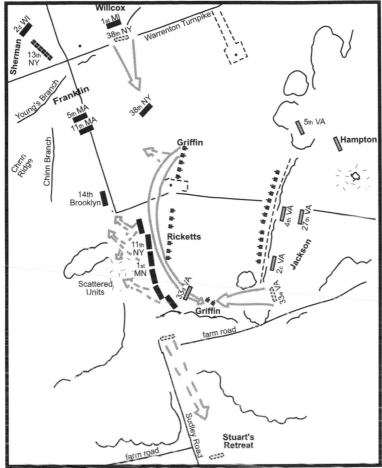

(After the second stage the action happened so quickly no exact time can be given.) The 38th New York arrives on the hill and is ordered to lie down behind Griffin's battery. In order to send a flanking fire down the Confederate left, Griffin moves two howitzers to the far right. Meanwhile, units from the 11th New York and 1st Minnesota return to the hill. Realizing his left flank was in imminent danger of being raked by cannon fire, Confederate Colonel Cummings orders the 33d Virginia to charge Griffin's two guns. They capture the guns, and the Union infantry scatter back down the hill. Union artillerymen manning Griffin's remaining three cannon take them down the hill to safety. Ricketts' battery stays.

*Colonel Cummings...seeing a battery of artillery
taking position and unlimbering, in close proxim-
ity and in a place where it could enfilade our troops,
determined to capture it before it could do any
damage...Then came the command: "Attention!
Forward march! Charge bayonets! Double quick!"
and away we went, sweeping everything before
us; but the enemy broke and fled.*[2]

Captain William Colvill, Jr., 1st Minnesota, saw the "...vol-
ley, which took effect in the centre of our regiment as well
as the batteries, killing our color sergeant, and wounding
three corporals of the color guard, and killing and wounding thirty men in the color company...the colors were riddled
with bullets."[3]

Near the Henry House, Ricketts urged the Zouaves to
help his artillerymen, but the Zouaves again "broke and ran."
Griffin rode down the hill to Young's Branch and sarcastically said to Major Barry, "Major, do you think the Zouaves
will support us?"

Barry replied, "I was mistaken."

Again Griffin exclaimed, "Do you think that was our
support?"

The major answered, "I was mistaken."

"Yes," said Griffin, "you were mistaken all around."[4]

Union reinforcements quickly arrived and the two captured Union cannon retaken (see map 7).

(Out of 95 men Griffin lost 27 killed, wounded, missing, and 55 missing horses, out of 101, most of which were
shot down during the battle.)

FOURTH STAGE

"Red-legged Devils"

Opposing Regiments

CONFEDERATE:	UNION:
33d Virginia	14th Brooklyn
450	640

As the Zouaves and Minnesota soldiers again streamed down the hill, the 14th Brooklyn (nicknamed the "Red-Legged Devils" because they wore red baggy pants) ran up through their retreating ranks. Although the 33d Virginia killed many Union soldiers and captured Griffin's two howitzers, the charge badly disorganized their ranks. At only forty yards from the 33d, the Brooklyn troops unleashed a volley of fire; the 33d Virginia's ranks crumbled. Outnumbered and unsupported they fell back behind Jackson's main line. The 14th Brooklyn recaptured Griffin's guns, and continued their assault (see map 8).

—MAP 8—
CONFEDERATE CANNON · FOURTH & FIFTH STAGE
STOP 5

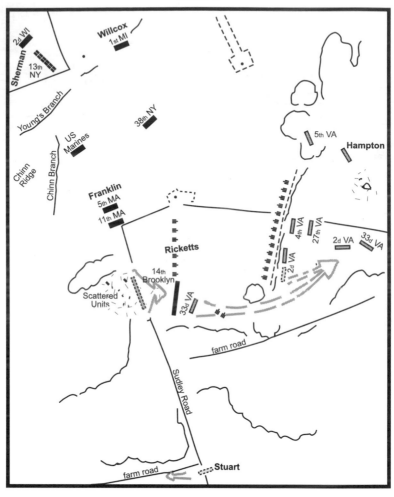

The 14th Brooklyn rushes up the hill and recaptures Griffin's two howitzers. Disorganized and outnumbered, the 33d Virginia retreats. In the confusion the 2d Virginia's left flank joins the 33d Virginia. Jackson's left flank crumbles.

Go to Stop 5: The Confederate cannon, southeast of the Henry House (see map 1, page ix)

FIFTH STAGE

"Few men can retire calmly under a galling fire..."
—Private George Baylor, 2d Virginia

Opposing Regiments

CONFEDERATE:	UNION:
2d Virginia	14th Brooklyn
300	640

As the 33d Virginia retreated, Colonel James Allen of the 2d Virginia directed Companies C and G to form a new line at a right angle to the rest of the regiment. While in the process of reforming, the 14th Brooklyn fired into their left flank. Private George Baylor later recalled:

Companies C and G, though suffering heavily, were unflinching and holding their own against largely superior numbers when the order was given to fall back and form a new line. This was done, no doubt, to present a front to the foe now outflanking us. It was, however, an unfor tunate move. Few men can retire calmly under a galling fire, and the ex- ecution of this order re- sulted in stampeding some good soldiers...[1]

Private George Baylor, age 19
2d Virginia, 300
Graduate of Dickinson College, 1860.

In the confusion many of the 2d Virginians misunderstood the order to reform; consequently, most of the 2d joined the retiring 33d. Jackson's left was crumbling. The men of the 14th Brooklyn, nevertheless, continued to concentrate their fire on the deadly Confederate artillery (see map 8). This gave Jackson time to call up his other regiments.

Return to Ricketts' battery (stop 3) near the Henry House

SIXTH STAGE

"Now d-damn you, take that."

—Private Bronson Gwynn, 4th Virginia

Opposing Regiments

CONFEDERATE:	UNION:
4th Virginia	14th Brooklyn
474	640
27th Virginia	
580	
49th Virginia Battalion	1st Michigan
210	500
6th North Carolina	
600	

To meet the threat in the center, Jackson quickly rode to the 4th and 27th Virginia and shouted, "Reserve your fire until they come within 50 yards, then fire and give them the bayonet, and when you charge, yell like furies."[2] Rising, the Virginians (joined by squads of men from the 2d and 33d Virginia) let loose a blood curdling scream and, with fixed bayonets, charged. (A Confederate described the rebel yell as, "Woh-who——ey! who——ey! who—ey! Woh-who—ey! who—ey! etc." The first syllable "woh" was short and low. "Who" was a very high and prolonged note deflecting upon "ey.")[3]

At the start, the 4th Virginia led the four deep line.[4] The regiments, however, became intermingled. Lieutenant Charles R. Norris, acting captain of Company B, 27th Virginia, shouted, "Come on, boys, quick, and we can whip them!!" Seconds later Norris dropped—shot through the upper left chest.[5] Private J.B. Caddall, of Company C, "Pulaski Guards," 4th Virginia, remembered:

> ...we were called to attention and ordered forward on the double-quick, and on an oblique move to the left over a stake and brush fence, through a skirt of pines and subject to a heavy fire of musketry. In a very few minutes we were in close contact with the ranks of the enemy of which a very conspicuous body was a Zouave Regiment from New York, with highly decorated uniforms, consisting of loosely fitting red breeches, blue blouses, with Turkish tassel as headgear.[6]

As the two sides collided, a vicious melée ensued. One Brooklynite jumped from behind a pine bush and lunged at Private Bronson Gwynn, 4th Virginia; the bayonet passed harmlessly through Bronson's coat between his arm and side. Gwynn pulled the bayonet from his coat and while firing his musket at the man's head stuttered, "Now d-damn you, take that," and rejoined his regiment near Ricketts' guns.[7]

Two other Confederates attacked Private Lewis Francis, 14th Brooklyn; one bayonetted him in the right knee. Private Francis later recalled the horrible incident:

> I was attacked by two rebel soldiers and wounded in the right knee with the bayonet. As I lay on the sod they kept bayoneting me until I received fourteen wounds. One then left me, the other remaining over me, when a Union soldier coming up, shot him in the breast, and he fell dead.[8]

(Amazingly, no vital organs were pierced, and he survived his wounds.)

The Virginia regiments suffered casualties as well. A musket ball struck Private William B. Ott, 4th Virginia, in the heart and killed him instantly; Sergeant James C. McKelsey, 33d Virginia, was killed, and Captain William

Lawrence Clark Jr., 2d Virginia, collapsed near the Henry House with a thigh wound.

Near the cannon Ricketts collapsed with a thigh wound. Without infantry support the remaining Union artillerymen retreated. One lieutenant, Doug Ramsay, ran past the "Alleghany Roughs," Company A, of the 27th Virginia. Private Clarence A. Fonerden of this company, took aim, but his comrade, Private William Fudge, fired first, killing Ramsay instantly (see map 9).[9] (In all, Ricketts' battery suffered 12 killed and 15 wounded out of approximately 94 artillerymen; the majority of artillery horses lay dead behind the cannon.)

Private Lewis Francis, age 42
Company I, 14th Brooklyn
A drawing sixteen months after a reamputation of his right hip, succeeding amputation for a bayonet stab wound through the right knee. He received at least fourteen stab wounds. One of the wounds involved his left testis, which was removed on July 24, 1861. He returned to Brooklyn and required the constant care of a nurse. He died suddenly May 31, 1874, around the age of 55.[10]

Sergeant James C. McKelsey
Company K, "The Shenandoah Sharpshooters," 33d Virginia
KIA

Captain William L. Clark, Jr., age 31
Company F, "Winchester Riflemen,"
2d Virginia
Yale University Graduate, 1849, and lawyer. Wounded around 3:00 p.m., his wound made him unfit for duty; he resigned April 14, 1862.

Lieutenant Charles Norris, age 17
Company B, 27th Virginia
Formerly a Virginia Military Institute Cadet, he was shot through the chest and killed. His coat is on display at the Manassas National Battlefield Park Visitor Center.

Lieutenant Doug Ramsay
Company I, 1st U.S. Artillery
Shot and killed while attempting to retreat. After the battle his body was stripped of all clothing except his socks.

—MAP 9—
HENRY HOUSE/RICKETTS' BATTERY · SIXTH STAGE
(Return to Stop 3)

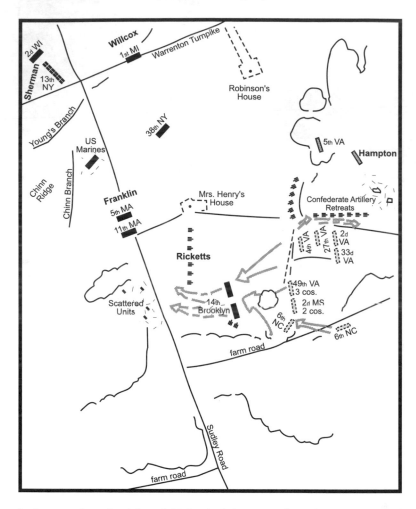

Jackson orders the 4th and 27th Virginia to attack (units from the 33d and 2d Virginia also join the assault). Three companies from the 49th Virginia Battalion, two companies from 2d Mississippi and the 6th North Carolina hit the 14th Brooklyn's right flank. The New Yorkers break and fall back. Meanwhile, the Confederate cannon are ordered off the field.

Return to Griffin's howitzers (Stop 4)

While the 4th and 27th Virginia assaulted Ricketts' battery, Colonel William Smith's Virginia battalion approached the hill. Yet, with only a small force, Smith's left flank was in danger of being turned. Fortunately for Smith, Colonel Charles Fisher's 6th North Carolina appeared on his left, hit the 14th Brooklyn's right flank and recaptured Griffin's two howitzers. The 14th's colonel, A.M. Wood, collapsed with a severe wound, and his men carried him to an ambulance; Private Augustus Brown fell dead, as did their color-bearer. Lieutenant Colonel E.B. Fowler assumed command of the regiment.

As the New Yorkers retreated they, and the newly arriving 1st Michigan, fired into the 6th North Carolina. In an attempt to rally his men, Colonel Fisher waved his sword, but a bullet struck him in the head, killing him instantly. The North Carolinians withdrew, yet Captain Isaac Avery quickly ordered a second charge; however, due to the confusion, only seven companies actively took part. The 6th again retook Griffin's guns and continued toward Ricketts'

Private Augustus
Brown, age 22
*Company C, 14th
Brooklyn; KIA*

Captain Isaac Avery,
age 33
*Company E, 6th
North Carolina*
(Seen in his colonel's
uniform)

Lieutenant Willie
Preston Mangum,
age 23
*Company B, 6th
North Carolina*
A musket ball struck him under his left arm. His Bible, which was in his left coat pocket, diverted the ball from his heart. He was, however, still severely wounded and died July 29, 1861.

battery; but the Union troops, who had scattered into the woods west of Sudley Road, fired into the 6th's left flank, and another group of soldiers fired into their rear. Avery was slightly wounded in the leg, and Lieutenant Willie P. Mangum toppled wounded in the side. Under this galling fire, and with their colonel dead, they fell back behind Jackson's brigade (see map 10). (The 6th North Carolina lost twenty-three killed and fifty wounded.)[11]

Go back to the Henry House

SEVENTH STAGE

Bayonets crossed...

Opposing Regiments

CONFEDERATE:	**UNION:**
27th Virginia	1st Michigan
580	500

After firing into the 6th North Carolina, half of the 1st Michigan charged into the Confederate line. The men crossed bayonets and swung clubbed muskets. Private Billy Cunningham, the color-bearer for the 1st Michigan, was shot and killed, and Private James Glenn of the 27th Virginia captured the 1st Michigan's flag. For the moment the Michigan soldiers had had enough, and they fell back to Sudley Road (see map 11).[12]

—MAP 10—
GRIFFIN'S TWO HOWITZERS · SIXTH STAGE, *continued*
(Return to Stop 4)

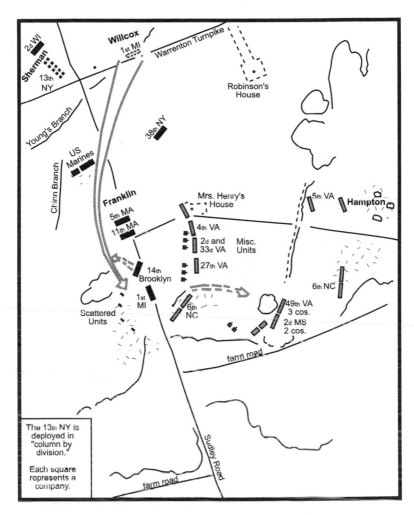

The 6th North Carolina recaptures Griffin's howitzers, but the 1st Michigan fires into their left flank. At the same time a group of unknown soldiers fires into the 6th's rear; they are forced to retreat.

—MAP 11—
HENRY HOUSE/RICKETTS' BATTERY · SEVENTH STAGE
(Return to Stop 3; remain here until the end.)

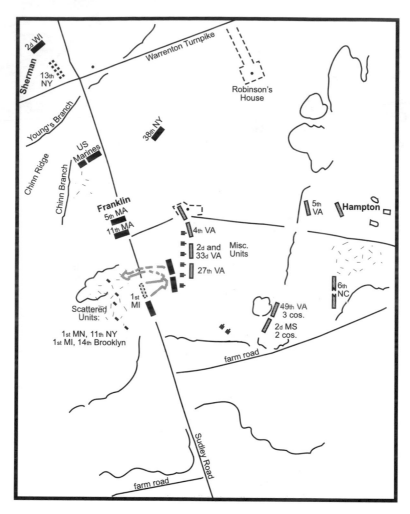

Due to confusion only half of the 1st Michigan charges up the hill. The 27th Virginia repulses their attack.

EIGHTH STAGE

"...a clear case...of self-imposed butchery."
—Private Fonerden, 27th Virginia

As the Michigan troops reorganized in the road, other soldiers from the 11th New York and 14th Brooklyn joined the 1st Michigan. Minutes later the make-shift battalion headed back up the hill. Private Fonerden, 27th Virginia, recalled:

> *...only a few moments later, what may be termed the slaughter of a regiment, or battalion of red-breeched Zouaves from Brooklyn, New York, immediately in front of the 27th Regiment, was a clear case, on their part, of self-imposed butchery. They had charged us to most uncomfortable nearness, pouring upon us their deadly fire, while their own loss was so great in actual dead it has often been said, one could walk on their dead bodies over a space of several acres without touching a foot upon the ground. That sight indeed was a dreadful one, and rendered ten-fold more conspicuous by the glittering of their bright red uniforms in the gleaming sun of that hot July.*[13]

Cut down by the musket fire, the Union make-shift battalion scattered down the hill, across the road and into the woods to the southwest (see map 12).

—MAP 12—
EIGHTH STAGE

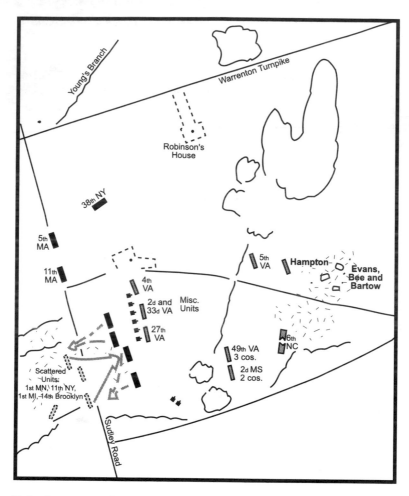

Units from several Union regiments attempt to recapture Ricketts' battery. Again, they are driven back.

NINTH STAGE

"...the sight of human agony"

—*Sergeant Henry N. Blake*

Opposing Regiments

CONFEDERATE:	UNION:
4th Virginia	5th Massachusetts
474	850
27th Virginia	11th Massachusetts
580	990

While remnants of the Union battalion (1st Michigan, 11th New York, 14th Brooklyn, and 1st Minnesota) mingled in the woods, two additional regiments attempted to retake the eight guns. Together the 5th and 11th Massachusetts numbered 1,840. The Massachusetts men climbed the road bank, aligned on the colors, and stormed up the hill. The Virginians fired; the 5th Massachusetts scattered; however, the 11th Massachusetts continued up the hill. Sergeant Henry N. Blake, 11th Massachusetts, recalled the ordeal:

> *...Two men placed their hands upon their ears to exclude the noise of the musketry and artillery, and rushed to the woods in the rear of the regiment...The shells struck rifles with such force, that some were twisted into the form of circles. A cannon-ball severed the arm of a sergeant, and threw it into the face of a soldier, who supposed, from the blow and the amount of blood upon his person, that he was dangerously wounded. One man stumbled over some briers while the column was ascending a hill; and a solid shot passed over him and killed his file-leader, when he fell upon the ground. The ghastly faces of the dead, and the sufferings of the wounded, who were begging for water, or imploring aid to be carried to the hospital, moved the hearts of men who had not by long experience become callous to the sight of human agony.*[14]

On the Confederate side, Private James W. Crowell, 4th Virginia, was killed, and under the weight of the attack the 4th and 27th Virginia retreated. Captain Thompson McAllister, commander of the "Alleghany Roughs," 27th Virginia, ordered the "men to fall back and rally...Every other man except the wounded and their attendants, rallied immediately some one hundred and fifty yards in the rear..."[15]

The 11th Massachusetts recaptured the eight prized cannon. Now they stood, dressed in gray, at the top of the hill near the guns (see map 13).

Sergeant Henry N. Blake,
age 22
Company K, 11th Massachusetts

Captain Thompson McAllister,
age 50
Company A, "Alleghany Roughs,"
27th Virginia

—MAP 13—
NINTH STAGE

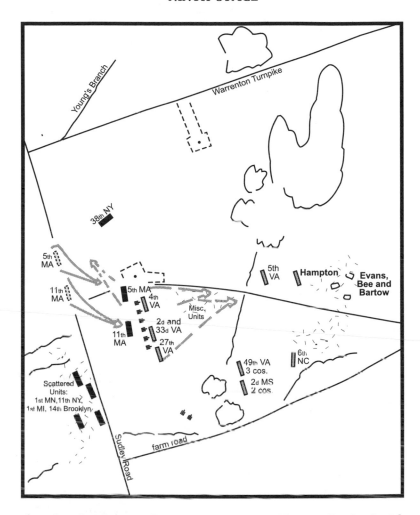

The 5th and 11th Massachusetts assault Henry Hill; immediately, the 5th breaks and retreats. The 11th Massachusetts, however, recaptures the cannon and for a second time Ricketts' battery is in Union hands. Dressed in their gray uniforms, the 11th Massachusetts awaits another Confederate counterattack.

TENTH STAGE

"...Come with me and go yonder where Jackson stands like a stone wall."

—*Brigadier General Barnard Bee*

Opposing Regiments

CONFEDERATE: **UNION:**

Hampton's Legion   11th Massachusetts
600   990

5th Virginia   Company I, 1st U.S. Artillery
380

With his center threatened, Beauregard rushed to the 5th Virginia and Hampton's Legion shouting, "Give them the bayonet."[16] The officers of the 5th cried out, "Close up, men!" "Steady there!" "Close up!"..."Forward!"[17]

Near Ricketts' cannon, the center of the 11th Massachusetts broke twice but reformed and held their position. Their right, however, was outflanked and forced to retreat. At the same time, Union troops to their rear, seeing the gray uniforms of the 11th, fired into their backs. Hit from the front, right, and rear the remaining soldiers of the 11th Massachusetts retreated.[18]

Black smoke covered the entire field; horses, men (dead and wounded), blanketed the ground. It was a chaotic scene. A bullet pierced Private William Woodward, 5th Virginia, and he fell near the Henry House. Woodward's friend, Private John Opie, saw another Confederate boy from Bee's brigade get hit in the forehead and fall without a groan. Opie reminisced:

> *He did not tell us his name, but simply asked if he could fall in with our company. Poor boy, he died among strangers like a hero. I felt like taking him in my arms, but that was no time for sentiment; besides, it was to be expected. [Another] fellow fell, shot on the eyebrow by a spent ball, making a slight wound, and, kicking and tossing his arms*

*about him, yelled, "O Lordy! I am killed! I am killed!
O Lordy, I am dead!" I saw the fellow was not hurt
much, only alarmed, and I said, "Poss," (as we
called him,) "are you really killed?" "Yes, O Lordy,
I am killed!" "Well," I said, "if you are really killed,
why in the devil don't you stop hallooing?" He is
alive to-day, but he never forgave me.*[19]

As the 5th Virginia ran into the midst of Ricketts' battery, their lieutenant colonel, William H. Harman, noticed the wounded Ricketts and said, "Why, Ricketts is this you?"

Captain Ricketts replied, "Yes, but I do not know you, sir."

"We were in the Mexican War together; Harman is my name." The captain then recognized the lieutenant colonel, and the two officers shook hands.

Not all the Confederates greeted Ricketts as cordially as Lieutenant Colonel Harman. So Ricketts would not be in the line of fire the Confederates removed him from the battlefield and placed him behind their lines. As he lay helpless a group of soldiers walked by and yelled, "Knock out his brains, the d——d Yankee." No one did harm Ricketts any further, but they did shake his nerves. After the battle the Confederates took him to Richmond. While Ricketts was a prisoner Colonel Wade Hampton visited him and treated him very well. He was released five months later, in December, and returned to the Union army.[20]

While the fighting raged near Mrs. Henry's house, Bee rushed to a Confederate unit behind the Robinson House and asked, "What regiment is this?"

Private William Woodward, age 30
5th Virginia
The night before the battle he stated to John Opie, "Boys, to-morrow I will be killed; but Opie you will survive the war!" Opie replied, "If you feel in this way, do not go into the battle." Woodward then said, "Yes, I will; I do not fear death. It is my destiny, and I will meet it like a man."[21]

Colonel Lucius J. Gartrell, age 40
Attended University of Georgia and Randolph-Macon. He was a U.S. Congressman; however, he supported states rights, and resigned from Congress when Georgia seceded. He led the 7th Georgia during the battle. He suffered a slight wound; his sixteen-year-old son, Henry, was killed.

Captain John Imboden, age 38
Held Bee's hand at his death bed.

Brigadier General Barnard Bee, age 37
Shot through the lower abdomen; died 4:00 a.m. July 22.

Colonel Francis Bartow, age 44
Struck just above his heart; he died shortly after being wounded.

A captain of the 4th Alabama replied, "Why, General, don't you know your own men?" "This is what is left of the 4th Alabama."

Surprised, Bee answered, "This is all of my brigade that I can find. Will you follow me back to where the fighting is going on?" The 4th complied and, pointing to his left, Bee shouted, "Come with me and go yonder where Jackson stands like a stone wall."[22] In the confusion the regiment became separated and only about twenty Alabamians followed their general. Orderly Sergeant William O. Hudson, 4th Alabama, heard Bee exclaim, "I am a dead man, I am shot." He reeled from his saddle; Hudson and his nephew, Private J.W. Hudson, caught Bee and placed him on the ground. With the help of their comrades they took the general to the pine and oak thicket. W.O. Hudson stripped down Bee's pants and found the bullet had passed through his abdomen. Hudson told him he "...feared his wound was mortal; but that he might live some days." The Alabama men then took him to a cabin at Manassas Junction; he died early the next morning, around 4 o'clock, while Captain John Imboden sat by his side holding his hand.[23]

At nearly the same time Bee fell, Colonel Francis Bartow suffered a mortal wound. While searching for reinforcements his horse had been shot from under him. Now, on foot, he led the 7th Georgia in the charge; the enemy fired, killing the 7th's color-bearer. Bartow picked up the flag and shouted, "On my boys—we will die rather than yield or retreat." At that moment a ball struck him in the left breast just above the heart. Fellow Georgians carried Bartow from the field and placed him on the ground. He then said, "They have killed me, my brave boys, but never give up the ship—we'll whip them yet," and then he died.[24] The 7th's colonel, Lucius Gartrell, went down as well. Lucius survived his wound but his sixteen-year-old son, Henry, was killed.

Although their officers fell at a frightful rate, the Alabamians, Mississippians, Georgians, Louisianans, and the 4th South Carolina continued to fight in the woods. On the Union side, men from the 1st Michigan, 1st Minnesota, 11th New York, and 14th Brooklyn fought the make-shift Confederate battalion (see map 14).

—MAP 14—
TENTH STAGE

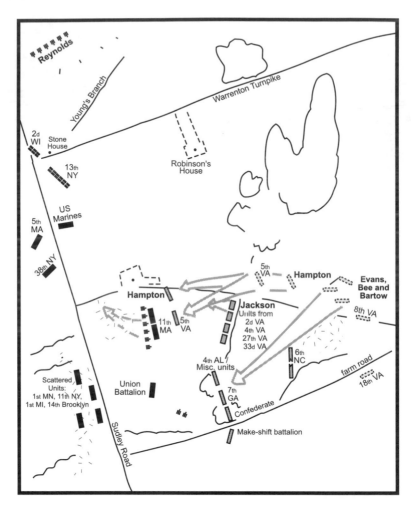

Jackson orders the 5th Virginia and Hampton's Legion to retake Ricketts'
battery. Other units from Jackson's brigade join in the assault. Fired upon
from the front and rear, the 11th Massachusetts retreats. To their right,
a Union battalion battles troops from Bee's and Bartow's brigades.

ELEVENTH STAGE

"Stop firing."

Opposing Regiments

CONFEDERATE:	UNION:
Hampton's Legion	13th New York
600	650

Ricketts' battery once again changed hands. Hiding behind the house, outhouse, sheds, bushes, caissons and cannon, the Virginians and South Carolinians awaited another Union assault. Within minutes Hampton's troops saw a regiment approaching their right flank.

The tenth Union regiment to assault the hill was the 13th New York of Colonel William T. Sherman's brigade. Advancing up the left slope of the hill, the 13th came within seventy yards of the house; there, the officers ordered the men to lie down and fire. A few Union soldiers, however, mistakenly thought the South Carolina Palmetto flag was an American flag. The New Yorkers yelled, "Stop firing." Hampton's right flank, on the other hand, did not hesitate; they poured a deadly volley into the New Yorkers. For nearly half-an-hour the 13th New York, lying in the tall grass, fought the South Carolinians (see map 15).[25]

—MAP 15—
ELEVENTH STAGE

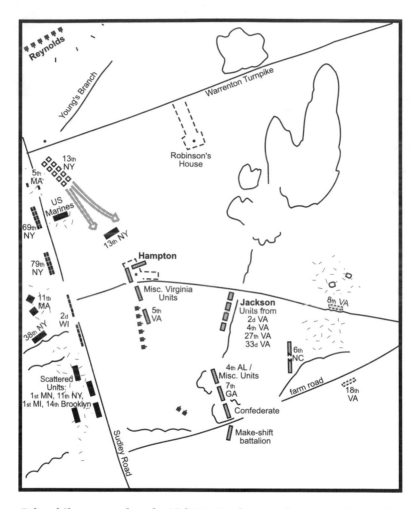

Colonel Sherman orders the 13th New York to attack. Approaching within seventy yards of the South Carolinians, the 13th hits the dirt and fights from a prone position for nearly half-an-hour.

TWELFTH STAGE

"O, my poor mother!"

—Corporal Willie Upham

Opposing Regiments

CONFEDERATE:	UNION:
Hampton's Legion	2d Wisconsin
600	900
5th Virginia	
380	

While the 13th New York dueled with Hampton's Legion on the Union far left, Colonel Sherman sent in his three remaining Union regiments piecemeal. The 2d Wisconsin, dressed in their militia gray, led the way.

As the Wisconsin boys waited on the Sudley Road they nervously joked and laughed. Now the time had come; with an Indian war whoop, the men jumped up and moved toward the Henry House. The Wisconsin lieutenant colonel, Harry Peck, wearing a red shirt, stood behind the right wing. Near the center, where the colors were unfurled, Major James Wadsworth, one of McDowell's staff officers, took charge. Major Duncan McDonald advanced behind the left wing.

From the start the 2d experienced trouble. In the confusion the regiment separated; the right wing, consisting of four companies, assaulted the Confederates near the woods, and the remaining six companies advanced up the hill near Ricketts' battery. On the right wing, many Wisconsin men dove behind dead horses and fired at the well hidden Confederates. Minutes later a Wisconsin officer ran down the rear of their right flank exclaiming, "For God's sake, stop firing, you are shooting friends."[26] Many Wisconsin boys hesitated, but the Confederates again fired and the duel resumed (see map 16). A ball went through Corporal Willie Upham's neck and exited out his back bone. As he fell he cried out, "Oh, my poor Mother!"[27] (Several of his comrades helped him to a field hospital where he was captured; he survived his wound.)

—MAP 16-
TWELFTH STAGE

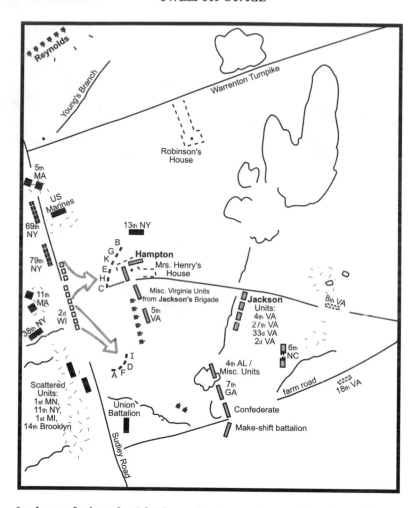

In the confusion, the 2d Wisconsin charges in two directions. The 5th Virginia, Hampton's Legion, and miscellaneous units from Jackson's other regiments, meet the attack.

Adding to the mayhem, the 79th and 69th New York, deployed on the Sudley Road, saw the Wisconsin gray uniforms and fired into their ranks. Near the house the left wing was also fired upon from three sides. The 2d rallied three times. Captain Andrew J. Langworthy, commanding Company K, later wrote about the terrible scene:

> ...all manner of projectiles known in warfare, shot, shell, grape, canister, musket and Minie balls, singing, screaming, rushing roaring in terrible discord, and sufficient to appall a stout heart, were turned upon us. On we dashed to their breastworks, the air fairly darkened with lead and iron. Engaging them face to face, although they had every advantage of us, being covered, yet when they rose to fire the steady aims of our 2d Wisconsin made fearful havoc in their ranks, and down they tumbled by hundreds, until a pile of dead and wounded "as high as huge Olympus" lay in their trenches. But for their terror here they would have killed every one of us. It was plainly visible in their faces as they rose to fire, and we were near enough to see it.[28]

Although Langworthy exaggerated the number of dead Confederates, both ranks could plainly see the fear on the men's faces and hear the orders for their deaths. Captain John Mansfield of Company G paced along his company and shouted, "Give it to 'em, boys!" "Give it to 'em!" "Down with their accursed flag!"

On the other side, some Wisconsin boys thought they heard the Virginians yell, "Kill them!" "Mow them down, the Northern Abolition sons of bitches!" "Give them no quarter!"[29]

The 2d, however, could not withstand salvos from three sides, and after ten to

Corporal Willie Upham, age 20
Company F, "Belle City Rifles,"
2d Wisconsin

—MAP 17—
TWELFTH STAGE, *continued*

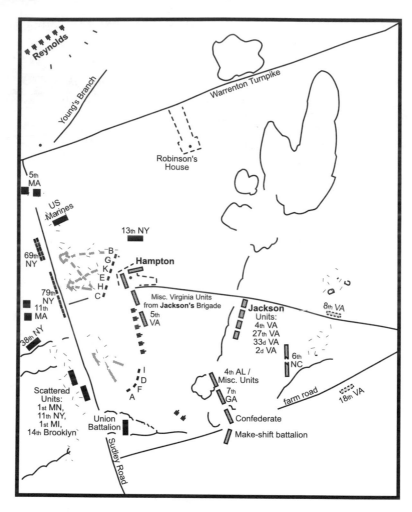

In another case of mistaken identity, Union troops, positioned behind the gray-clad 2d Wisconsin, fire into their backs. Struck from the front and rear, the 2d is compelled to retreat.

fifteen minutes they retreated to Sudley Road (see map 17). (During the battle, the 2d Wisconsin lost 24 killed, 65 wounded and 23 missing.)

Afterward, dissatisfied with the leadership of their commanders during the conflict, the Wisconsin captains invited Colonel Coon, Lieutenant Colonel Peck, and Major McDonald to resign. The three willingly and quickly complied.[30]

THIRTEENTH STAGE

"Come on, my brave Highlanders!"

—Colonel James Cameron, 79th New York

Opposing Regiments

CONFEDERATE:	UNION:
Hampton's Legion	79th New York Highlanders
600	"Highlanders"
	895
5th Virginia	
380	

As the 2d Wisconsin fell back, Sherman ordered the 79th New York into the fray. In the confusion many Wisconsin soldiers joined the New York regiment. The 79th's commander, Colonel James Cameron, placed himself to the right front and shouted, "Come on, my brave Highlanders!" One Highlander, Private William Todd, later described the attack:

When half way up the hill, on the brow of which the enemy was posted, we received his first volley, and many of our comrades fell. This threw us into some confusion, but under the directions of our officers we reformed and pressed on, delivering our fire and receiving another murderous volley, in return, by which Colonel Cameron was killed [he was shot through the chest]; this, with the constant fire of shells from their batteries, somewhat

*staggered us, but reforming we again pressed
forward...Suddenly some one cried out, "Cease firing! you're shooting your own men!" "No they ain't!"
another replied; "don't you see they are firing at
us?"...Contradictory orders again rang out—"Blaze
away, boys! they're only trying to deceive us!"
"Cease firing, I tell you! They are our own men!"
By this time the line on the hill-top had formed and
all doubt as to their identity vanished. "Ready! aim!
fire!" came from that column, and a shower of bullets crashed through our already torn and bleed-
ing ranks!*[31]

A Wisconsin corporal clearly remembered his experience. "I
went up past the tall rebel whom I had shot through the
breast about a second or so after he had hurrahed for
Beauregard, and whose great blue eyes stared so wildly that
I think of them often still, and presume I always shall."[32]

The 79th New York and remnants of the 2d Wisconsin
wavered, tried to rally, but the Virginians and South Carolinians sent another lethal volley into their ranks. The men
fell back to the road and sought shelter from the deadly

A nineteenth-century artist's rendition of the Highlanders at Bull Run
and Colonel Cameron's death.

musketry (see map 18). (Thirty-two Highlanders were killed, 51 wounded and 115 were missing.)

On the Confederate side, Hampton's Legion and the 5th Virginia beat back four Union regiments in nearly forty minutes of fighting. Hampton lay near the Henry House with slight head and ankle wounds. (The bullet grazed his left temple.) Captain James Conner assumed command of the Legion. The Confederates were extremely thirsty and tired when two fresh Union regiments charged into their ranks.

FOURTEENTH STAGE

"Come on, boys! you have got your chance at last."
—Captain Thomas Meagher, 69th New York

Opposing Regiments

CONFEDERATE:	UNION:
Hampton's Legion 600	69th New York "Irish" Regiment 998
5th Virginia 380	38th New York "Second Scott Life Guard" 665

Sherman's last unscathed regiment was the 69th New York. Stripped of their knapsacks and overcoats, the Irishmen, joined by the 38th New York, rushed up the hill. Captain Thomas Meagher rode at the head of the 69th shouting, "Come on, boys! you have got your chance at last."[33] His company, a special Zouave detachment, along with the other Irishmen, surged forward.

Confederate Lieutenant Richard Lewis, a member of a 4th South Carolina company which had become intermingled with Hampton's Legion, recalled:

Our company was lying behind the plank and rail fence in front of the Henry house at one time in the

—MAP 18—
THIRTEENTH STAGE

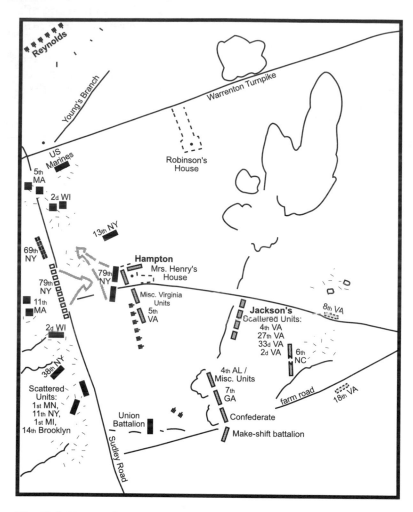

The 79th New York Highlanders assault Henry Hill; their colonel, James Cameron, is killed. With the death of their colonel, the Highlanders retreat.

*fight, and the enemy commenced shelling us furi-
ously, and the Yankee Zouaves, who were dressed
in red, commenced charging us and they scared
us pretty badly. We started to run, but Captain
Kilpatrick drew his sword and ordered us to lie
down, and said if any of us ran he would hew us
down; but Johnson Wright, his negro, who had been
with us fighting up to that time, was lying behind
the rail fence, when a shell struck the fence and
knocked a rail off on him. Kilpatrick's sword never
reached him, for he says he never stopped long
enough to get his breath between there and
Manassas Junction.*[34]

The South Carolinians held their position momentarily, but
under the combined weight of the infantry and artillery they
finally retreated to the pine trees.

On the Union right, Colonel Hobart Ward, 38th New
York, quickly detailed several of his men to pull three cannon off the hill. The New Yorkers managed to drag the guns
back three-hundred yards to Sudley Road. Meanwhile, Ward
saw to the right the make-shift Union battalion scatter from
the woods. At double-quick the 38th rushed into the woods.
Joined by fragments of the 1st Michigan, 1st Minnesota,
14th Brooklyn, and 11th New York, the Union battalion en-
gaged in a "sharp and spirited" skirmish (see map 19).[35]
Outnumbered, the Confederates fell back, and once again
Henry Hill was recaptured. To many Union troops it seemed
the field had been won. The Confederate commanders, however, refused to call a general retreat. Instead, they pushed
forward two fresh regiments.

—MAP 19—
FOURTEENTH STAGE

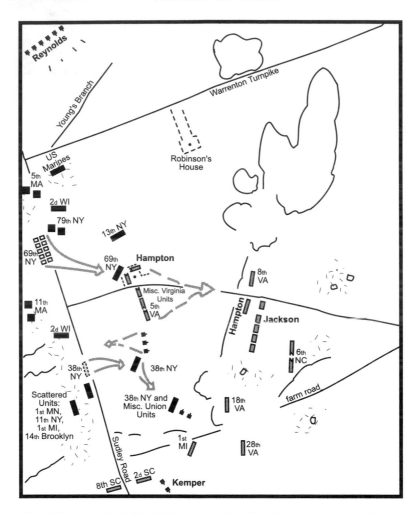

The 69th New York "Irish" Regiment breaks through the Confederate line. On the 69th's right flank, the 38th New York, 1st Michigan, and miscellaneous Union units, battle in the woods.

FIFTEENTH STAGE

"...remember Ireland and Fontenoy."
—*Captain Thomas Meagher, 69th New York*

Opposing Regiments

CONFEDERATE:	UNION:
8th Virginia	13th New York 650
Hampton's Legion 600	69th New York 998
18th Virginia	38th New York 665
2d South Carolina	

While Ward's regiment skirmished in the woods, the 69th continued up the slope of Henry Hill. Using the pine trees as cover, the Confederates showered the Irishmen with lead. The Irish Brigade historian recounted:

> *After each repulse, the regiment formed and charged right up on the batteries, Meagher's company of Zouaves suffered desperately, their red dress making them a conspicuous mark for the enemy. When Meagher's horse was torn from under him by a rifled cannon ball, he jumped up, waved his sword, and exclaimed, "Boys! look at that flag—remember Ireland and Fontenoy."... Colonel Corcoran rallied and charged with them in every assault.[36]*

To counter this attack, Captain Conner redeployed Hampton's Legion to the right of Colonel Robert E. Withers' 18th Virginia. Withers rode to a group of officers situated behind his regiment; there he asked Beauregard for orders.

---

* Remember, Hampton's Legion had been fighting since 11:30 a.m, and they had been suffering casualties almost the entire time. It was now about 3:45–4:00 p.m.

The general stated, "Change your direction to the left oblique and charge across the Sudley Road."[37] Confronted by the combined force of the 8th and 2d South Carolina, 18th Virginia, Hampton's Legion, and the 8th Virginia, the thirteen Union regiments—disorganized and scattered from the Henry House to Sudley Ford—began leaving the field (see map 20). The Confederates, after approximately two hours, regained control of the hill and eight of the prized Union cannon.

Captain Thomas Meagher, age 37
Company K, 69th New York

—MAP 20—
FIFTEENTH STAGE

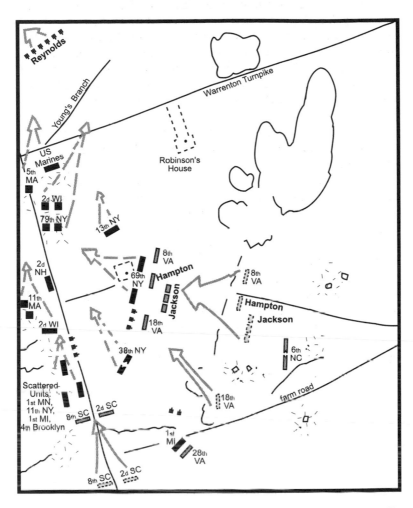

Confederate reinforcements arrive and push the Union regiments off Henry Hill. The Union troops around the hill begin a general retreat.

CASUALTIES ON HENRY HILL:

Nearly 193 Confederates were killed and another 326 wounded. The Union suffered 285 killed and 647 wounded—in all, 1,452 Americans lay in and around the plateau, Mrs. Henry included. Approximately 104 artillery horses from Griffin's and Ricketts' batteries were also killed or wounded.

The 33d Virginia suffered 146 killed and wounded out of 400, the heaviest Confederate casualties during the Henry Hill fighting.

Colonel Gorman's 1st Minnesota sustained the highest Union casualties. Out of 900 men, 150 were either killed or wounded.

As the Union regiments retreated from Henry Hill the battle shifted to the Chinn farm area and lasted for another half-hour; it finally ended around 4:30 p.m. The exhausted Union troops limped back to Washington. Tired Confederate soldiers collapsed and slept among the dead. Others looked for a fallen comrade.

In only ten-and-a-half hours 900 Americans fell in and around Matthews Hill, John Dogan's farm, Young's Branch, Henry Hill, and the Chinn farm.

The Battle of First Manassas (Bull Run) was the "*ultima ratio* of force; and the sword having now been drawn in earnest,...[the war had to] be fought out."[38]

Confederate:	K	W	Union:	K	W
Hampton's Legion	19	100	2d Maine	13	24
5th Virginia	6	47	3d Connecticut	4	13
4th Virginia	31	100	11th New York	48	75
2d Virginia	18	72	14th Brooklyn	23	48
27th Virginia	19	122	1st Minnesota	42	108
33d Virginia	45	101	1st Michigan	6	37
6th North Carolina	23	50	5th Massachusetts	5	26
8th Virginia	6	23	11th Massachusetts	8	40
18th Virginia	6	13	13th New York	11	27
28th Virginia	0	9	2d Wisconsin	24	65
49th Virginia Battalion	10	30	79th New York	32	51
2d South Carolina	6	43	69th New York	38	59
8th South Carolina	5	23	38th New York	15	55
4th Alabama (about 20)*			U.S. Marine Battalion	9	19
4th South Carolina (a few)*					

* The 4th Alabama and 4th South Carolina sustained their heaviest losses during the morning fight on Matthews Hill.

Notes

Introduction

1. Due to mismanagement of his army McDowell only utilized between 13,000–15,000 men. The remaining troops he either did not effectively use or many dropped out, too exhausted from marching, or they were held in reserve.

2. The actual Confederate troops directly involved in the fighting numbered approximately 14,050. The other troops either arrived too late or were guarding the right flank.

Stop 1

1. John D. Imboden, "Incidents of the First Bull Run," *Battles and Leaders*, ed. Robert U. Johnson and Clarence C. Buel, Vol. I (New York: Castle, 1888), 234. Hereinafter cited as *B&L*.

2. Lieutenant Colonel G.F.R. Henderson, *Stonewall Jackson and the American Civil War*, Vol. I (Secaucus, New Jersey: Blue and Grey), 145.

3. John Hennessy, *The First Battle of Manassas: An End To Innocence July 18–21, 1861* (Lynchburg, Virginia: H.E. Howard, Inc., 1989), 69.

4. *The War of the Rebellion: A Compilation of the Official Records of the Union and Confederate Armies*, Series I, Vol. II (Washington D.C., Government Printing Office, 1880–1901), 187. Hereinafter cited as O.R.

5. Jackson adopted this reverse slope tactic from the Duke of Wellington (Arthur Welleseley), who effectively used this tactic in several of his battles, see Henderson, 146.

6. Beauregard, "The First Battle of Bull Run," *B&L*, Vol. I, p. 211. See also Hennessy, 71.

7. *B&L*, Vol. I, 211.

8. Brevet Major General James B. Fry, "McDowell's Advance to Bull Run," *B&L*, Vol. I, 187.

9. William T. Sherman, *Memoirs of General William T. Sherman* (New York: Da Capo, 1984), 183.

10. Ibid., 188.

11. William Todd, *Seventy-Ninth Highlanders* (Albany: Brandow, Barton and Co., 1886), 34. See also, Henry N. Blake, *Three Years In The Army Of the Potomac* (Boston: Lee and Shepard, 1865), 16.

12. Hennessy, 74.

Stop 2

1. O.R., Vol. II, 353.

2. James H. Mundy, *Second to None: The Story of the 2d. Maine Volunteers "The Bangor Regiment"* (Scarborough, Maine: Harp Publications, 1992), 70–71. See also O.R., Vol. II, 353.

3. Ibid., 66–67.

4. William C. Davis, *Battle at Bull Run: A History of the First Major Campaign of the Civil War* (Garden City, New York: Doubleday and Company, Inc., 1977), 233. For the "Yankee Yell" see R.L.T. Beale, *History of the Ninth Virginia Cavalry in the War Between the States* (Richmond: B.F. Johnson Publishing Co., 1899), 191.

5. O.R., Vol. II, 567. See also Hennessy, 75.

6. O.R., Vol. II, 353. For information concerning the 2d Maine see Mundy, 73–75.

Stop 3

1. *Report of the Joint Committee on the Conduct of the War, In Three Parts: Bull Run to Ball's Bluff*, Part II (Washington: Government Printing Office, 1863), 169. Hereafter cited *CCW*.

2. Ibid., 243.

3. *B&L*, 234. Helena Huntington Smith, "At the Eye of the Hurricane," *First Manassas (Bull Run) and the war around it...* (Manassas: First Manassas Corporation, 1961), 19–20 & 57–59. See also Joseph Mills Hanson, *Bull Run Remembers...The History, Traditions and Landmarks of the Manassas (Bull Run) Campaigns Before Washington 1861–1862* (Manassas: National Capitol Publisher, Inc., 1953), 88–89 and Hennessy, 79. Hanson's account differs with Smith's. He states Rosa Stokes was Mrs. Henry's maid and that Rosa was wounded in the ankle.

4. *CCW*, 220.

5. Ibid., 219.

6. James I. Robertson, Jr., *The Stonewall Brigade* (Baton Rouge: Louisiana State University Press, 1963), 38. See also J.B. Caddall, 4th Regiment, in *Richmond Times-Dispatch*, November 27, 1904.

7. Henderson, 147.

8. John O. Casler, *Four Years in the Stonewall Brigade* (Girard, Kansas: Appeal Publishing Co., 1906), 27.

9. Hennessy, 80.

10. Private Lewis Herbert Metcalf, "So Eager Were We All..." *American Heritage*, Vol. XVI, no. 4 (June 1965): 37.

11. Harrison H. Comings, *Personal Reminiscences of Company E, New York Fire Zouaves, Bettter Known As Ellsworth's Fire Zouaves.* Found at U.S. Military History Institute, Archives Division, Carlisle, Pennsylvania.

12. Sergeant John G. Merritt, "A Minnesota Boy's First Battle," *Sabre and Bayonet: Stories of Heroism and Military Adventure*, ed. Theo. F. Rodenbough (New York: G.W. Dillingham Co., 1897), 41.

13. William White Blackford, *War Years With Jeb Stuart* (New York: Charles Scribner's Sons, 1945), 30.

Stop 4

1. *CCW*, 169.

2. Casler, 27.

3. William Lochren, "Narrative of the First Regiment," *Minnesota in the Civil and Indian Wars, 1861–1865,* Vol. I (St. Paul: Pioneer Press Co., 1891), 9–10.

4. *CCW*, 169.

Stop 5

1. George Baylor, *Bull Run to Bull Run; Or, Four Years in the Army of Northern Virginia* (Washington, D.C.: Zenger Publishing Co., Inc., 1900), 22. Baylor graduated from Dickinson College in 1860.

2. Hennessy, 97.

3. Beale, 192.

4. J.B. Caddall, "The Pulaski Guards. Company C, 4th Virginia Infantry, at the First Battle of Manassas, July 21, 1861," *Southern Historical Society Papers*, Vol. 32, 175.

5. Lowell Reidenbaugh, *27th Virginia Infantry* (Lynchburg, Virginia: H.E. Howard, 1993), 166.

6. Caddall, *Southern Historical Society Papers*, Vol. 32, 176.

7. William Gleason Bean, *The Liberty Hall Volunteers: Stonewall's College Boys* (Charlottesville: The University Press of Virginia, 1964), 45–46.

8. "Documents," in *The Rebellion Record*, Vol. 4., 533–534. For a detailed account of Private Lewis Francis' wounds see, *The Medical and Surgical History of the War of the Rebellion*, Part III, Vol. II., 154.

9. Concerning William Ott's death see, Ted Barclay's, *Liberty Hall Volunteers, Letters From the Stonewall Brigade (1861–1864)*, ed. Charles W. Turner (Berryville: Rockbridge Publishing Co., 1992), 25. For William L. Clark, Jr.'s wound refer to Dennis E. Frye's, *2nd Virginia* (Lynchburg: H.E. Howard, 1984), 89. Lieutenant Doug Ramsay's death can be found in Clarence Albert Fonerden's, *A Brief History of the Military Career of Carpenter's Battery* (New Market, Virginia: Henkel and Company, 1911), 11.

10. "Documents," in *The Rebellion Record*, Vol. 4., 533.

11. Walter Clark, ed., *Histories of the Several Regiments and Battalions from North Carolina in the Great War 1861–'65*, Vol. I (Wendell, North Carolina: Broadfoot, 1982), 297–99 and pp. 340–46; Vol. V., 29–33 and 581–85. See also Iobst, 20–28.

   There is some debate among the 6th North Carolina concerning who fired upon their rear ranks. Some speculate it was the 4th Alabama. Major Isaac Avery theorized it was the 11th Massachusetts, wearing gray uniforms, and mistakenly identified as Confederate troops.

12. Fonerden, 12. See also Robert C. Wallace, *A Few Memories Of A Long Life*, ed. John M. Carroll (Fairfield, Washington: Ye Galleon Press, 1988), 14.

13. Fonerden, 13.

14. Henry N. Blake, *Three Years in the Army of the Potomac* (Boston: Lee and Shepard, 1865), 23.

15. J. Gray McAllister, *Sketch of Captain Thompson McAllister, Citizen, Soldier, Christian* (Petersburg: Penn & Owen, 1896), 16–17.

16. Hennessy, 101.

17. John N. Opie, *A Rebel Cavalryman With Lee, Stuart and Jackson* (Chicago: W.B. Conkey Co., 1899), 34.

18. Gustavus B. Hutchinson, *A Narrative of the Formation and Services of the Eleventh Massachusetts Volunteers, From April 15, 1861, to July 14, 1865* (Boston: Alfred Mudge and Son, 1893), 24.

19. Opie, 32.

20. Ibid., 34; *CCW*, 244, and "Documents," *The Rebellion Record*, Vol. 4., 533.

21. Opie, 26.

22. R.T. Coles, 23 and 237; In *Our Living And Our Dead: Devoted to North Carolina—Her Past, Her Present And Her Future* (Raleigh: Southern Historical Society, September 1874 to February 1875), Vol. I, 564. William O. Hudson, 4th Alabama, remembered Bee said, "follow me, let us support Jackson; see he stands like a stone wall." See also, Hennessy, 83. Tradition has always portrayed Bee stating this as his units were retreating from Matthews Hill and just as Jackson's brigade arrived. His statement, however, does not make sense at this time. As soon as Jackson arrived on Henry Hill he ordered his men to lie down and protect themselves from the Union artillery shells. They were neither standing or fighting. For more information see Hennessy, 152 endnote 52.

23. *Our Living And Our Dead*, Vol. I., 564. See also *B&L*, Vol. 1, 237. See letter of W.A. Evans, in Maud Morrow Brown's, *The University Greys: Co. A Eleventh Mississippi Regiment Army of Northern Virginia 1861–1865* (Richmond: Garrett and Massie Inc., 1940), 18–19.

24. *Savannah Republican*, August 1, 1861.

25. Hennessy, 103. Sherman, 183–184.

26. Brigadier General Thomas S. Allen, "The Second Wisconsin At the First Battle of Bull Run," *War Papers: Being Papers Read Before the Commandery of the State of Wisconsin, Military Order of the Loyal Legion of the United States*, Vol. I (Wilmington: Broadfoot Publishing Company, 1993), 389.

27. Gaff, 210.

28. Ibid., 223.

29. Ibid., 224.

30. George H. Otis, *The Second Wisconsin Infantry*, ed. Alan D. Gaff (Dayton, Ohio: Morningside, 1984), 39.

31. Todd, *The Seventy-ninth Highlanders*, 37–38.

32. Gaff, 227.

33. Captain D.P. Conyngham, A.D.C., *The Irish Brigade and Its Campaigns: With Some Account of the Corcoran Legion, and Sketches of the Principal Officers* (Boston: Patrick Donahoe, 1869), 43.

34. Lieutenant Richard Lewis, *Camp Life of a Confederate Boy, Of Bratton's Brigade, Longstreet's Corps, C.S.A.* (Charleston: News and Courier Book Presses, 1883), 13–14.

35. O.R., Vol. II, 415.

36. Conyngham, 37.

37. Robert E. Withers, M.D., *Autobiography of an Octogenarian* (Roanoke: Stone Printing and MFG. Co. Press, 1907), 149.

38. *The Rebellion Record*, Vol. II., 113.

Photographs—Bibliography
(In order of appearance)

Abbreviations:

Miller: Francis T. Miller, *The Photographic History of The Civil War.* 10 vols. New York: The Review of Reviews Co., 1912.

MNP: Manassas National Park. Museum Director, Jim Burgess.

USAMHI: United States Army Military History Institute. Photo archivists, Mike Winey and Randy Hackenburg.

Capt. John Imboden, USAMHI.

Brigadier General Thomas Jackson, USAMHI.

Robinson's House, USAMHI.

Capt. James B. Ricketts, USAMHI.

Capt. Charles Griffin, USAMHI.

Drawing of Mrs. Henry's house by Fremaux, Nelson Coll. via USAMHI.

Pvt. John Casler, *Four Years in the Stonewall Brigade*, 1906.

Col. William Gorman, USAMHI.

Col. Noah Farnham, USAMHI.

Sgt. John G. Merritt, USAMHI.

Sudley Road, USAMHI.

Pvt. George Baylor, May Morris Room, Dickinson College Library.

Pvt. Lewis Francis, *The Medical and Surgical History of the War of the Rebellion*, Part 3, Vol. II., 1883, page 154.

Sgt. James C. McKelsey, MNP.

Capt. William L. Clark, Jr., Herren Coll. via USAMHI.

Lt. Charles Norris, MNP.

Lt. Doug Ramsay, Borrell, Sr., Coll. via USAMHI.

Pvt. Augustus Brown, USAMHI.

Capt. Isaac Avery, *Histories of the Several Regiments and Battalions from North Carolina in the Great War 1861–1865*, Vol. I., 1901.

Lt. Willie Mangum, Ibid.

Sgt. Henry Blake, USAMHI.

Capt. Thompson McAllister, *Sketch of Captain Thompson McAllister, Citizen, Soldier, Christian*, 1896.

Pvt. William Woodward, *A Rebel Cavalryman...*, 1899.

Col. Lucius J. Gartrell, Miller, Vol. 10.

Brig. Gen. Barnard Bee, USAMHI.

Col. Francis Bartow, USAMHI.

Corp. Willie Upham, *Racine County Militant* (1915) via Racine Heritage Museum, Racine, Wisconsin.

A drawing of Colonel Cameron's death, *The Seventy-Ninth Highlanders*, 1886.

Capt. Thomas Meagher, USAMHI.

Bibliography

Alexander, Edward P. *Fighting for the Confederacy: The Personal Recollections of General Edward Porter Alexander.* Ed. Gary W. Gallagher. Chapel Hill: The University of North Carolina Press, 1989.

――― "The Battle of Bull Run." *Scribners Magazine.* Vol. XLI (1907), pp. 80–94.

Allen, Thomas S. "The Second Wisconsin at the First Battle of Bull Run." *War Papers Read Before the Commandery of the State of Wisconsin, Military Order of the Loyal Legion of the United States.* Vol. I. Milwaukee: Burdick, Amitage & Allen, 1891.

Barclay, Ted. *Letters from the Stonewall Brigade (1861–1864).* Ed. Charles W. Turner, Berryville, Virginia: Rockbridge Publishing Co., 1992.

Baylor, George. *Bull Run to Bull Run; Or, Four Years in the Army of Northern Virginia.* Washington, D.C.: Zenger Publishing Co., Inc., 1900.

Beale, R.L.T. *History of the Ninth Virginia Cavalry, In the War Between the States.* Richmond: B.F. Johnson Publishing Co., 1899.

Bean, William G. *The Liberty Hall Volunteers: Stonewall's College Boys.* Charlottesville: The University Press of Virginia, 1964.

Beauregard, P.G.T. *A Commentary on the Campaign and Battle of Manassas of July 1861 Together With a Summary of the Art of War.* New York: Putnams, 1891.

――― . "The First Battle of Bull Run." *Battles and Leaders Of the Civil War*, Vol. I, pp. 196–227.

Blackford, William W. *War Years With Jeb Stuart.* New York: Charles Scribner's Sons, 1945.

Blake, Henry N. *Three Years In the Army of the Potomac.* Boston: Lee and Shepard, 1865.

Boatner, Mark M. *The Civil War Dictionary.* New York: Vintage Books, 1991.

Caddall, J.B. "The Pulaski Guards. Company C, 4th Virginia Infantry, at the First Battle of Manassas, July 21, 1861." *Southern Historical Society Papers.* Vol. 32, pp. 174–78.

Casler, John O. *Four Years in the Stonewall Brigade.* Girard, Kansas: Appeal Publishing Co., 1906.

Clark, Walter, ed. *Histories of the Several Regiments and Battalions from North Carolina in the Great War 1861–1865.* 5 vols. Goldsboro, North Carolina: Nash Brothers, Book and Job Printers, 1901.

Coles, R.T. *From Huntsville to Appomattox: R.T. Coles's History of 4th Regiment, Alabama Volunteer Infantry, C.S.A. Army of Northern Virginia.* Jeffrey D. Stocker, ed. Knoxville: The University of Tennessee Press, 1996.

Comings, Harrison H. *Personal Reminiscences of Company E, New York Fire Zouaves, Better Known As Ellsworth's Fire Zouaves.* Malden, Massachusetts: J. Gould Tilden, Steam Book, 1886. Found at U.S. Military History Institute, Archives Division, Carlisle, Pennsylvania.

Conrad, D.B. "History of the First Battle of Manassas and the Organization of the Stonewall Brigade." *Southern Historical Society Papers.* Vol. 19, pp. 88–94.

Conyngham, D.P. *The Irish Brigade and Its Campaigns: With Some Account of the Corcoran Legion, and Sketches of the Principal Officers.* Boston: Patrick Donahoe, 1869.

Cudworth, Warren H. *History of the First Regiment (Massachusetts Infantry).* Boston: Walker, Fuller, and Co., 1866.

Cummings, Arthur C. "Thirty-third Virginia at Manassas." *Southern Historical Society Papers.* Vol. 34, pp. 363–71.

Cunningham, Horace H. *Field Medical Services at the Battles of Manassas.* Athens: University of Georgia Press, 1968.

Davis, Jefferson. *The Rise and Fall of the Confederate Government.* 2 vols. New York: D. Appleton and Co., 1881.

Davis, William C. *Battle at Bull Run: A History of the First Major Campaign of the Civil War.* Garden City, New York: Doubleday and Company Inc., 1977.

————. *First Blood: Fort Sumter to Bull Run.* Alexandria: Time-Life Books, 1983.

First Manassas (Bull Run) And the War Around It.... Manassas: First Manassas Corp., 1961.

Fonerden, C.A. *A Brief History of the Military Career of Carpenter's Battery.* New Market: Henkel and Co., 1911.

Freeman, Douglas S. *Lee's Lieutenants: A Study in Command.* 3 Vols. New York: Charles Scribner's Sons, 1942.

Fry, James B. "McDowell's Advance To Bull Run." *Battles and Leaders of the Civil War,* Vol. I, pp. 167–93.

————. *McDowell and Tyler in the Campaign of Bull Run, 1861.* New York: Van Nostrand, 1884.

Frye, Dennis E. *2nd Virginia Infantry.* Lynchburg, Virginia: H.E. Howard, 1984.

Gaff, Alan D. *If this is War: A History of the Campaign of Bull's Run by the Wisconsin Regiment Thereafter Known as the Ragged Ass Second.* Dayton: Morningside, 1991.

Hanson, Joseph M. *Bull Run Remembers...The History, Traditions and Landmarks of the Manassas (Bull Run) Campaigns Before Washington 1861–1862.* Manassas: National Capitol Publisher Inc., 1953.

Henderson, G.F.R. *Stonewall Jackson and the American Civil War.* 2 Vols. Secaucus, New Jersey: Blue and Grey.

Henderson, Lindsey P. *The Oglethorpe Light Infantry.* Savannah and Chatham County, Georgia: The Civil War Centennial Commission, 1961.

Hennessy, John. *The First Battle of Manassas: An End To Innocence July 18–21.* Lynchburg, Virginia: H.E. Howard, Inc., 1989.

————. "The First Hour's Fight On Henry Hill." 1985. Manassas National Park Archives.

Holcombe, Return I. *History of the First Regiment Minnesota Volunteer Infantry: 1861–1865.* Minnesota: Easto and Masterman, 1916.

Hundley, George A. "Beginning and the Ending." *Southern Historical Society Papers.* Vol. 23, 1896.

Hutchinson, Gustavus B. *A Narrative of the Formation and Services of the Eleventh Massachusetts Volunteers, From April 15, 1861, to July 14, 1865.* Boston: Alfred Mudge and Son, 1893.

Imboden, John D. "Incidents of the First Bull Run." *Battles and Leaders.* Vol. I. Robert U. Johnson and Clarence C. Buel, eds. New York: Castle, 1888.

Imholte, John Q. *The First Volunteers: History of the First Minnesota Volunteer Regiment 1861–1865.* Minneapolis: Ross and Haines, 1963.

Iobst, Richard W. *The Bloody Sixth: The Sixth North Carolina Regiment Confederate States of America.* Raleigh: Christian Printing Co., 1965.

Irby, Richard. *Historical Sketch of the Nottoway Grays.* Richmond: J.W. Fergusson & Son, 1878.

Johnston, Joseph E. "Responsibilities of the First Bull Run." *Battles and Leaders.* Robert U. Johnson and Clarence C. Buel, ed. New York: Castle, 1888.

Johnston, Robert M. *Bull Run: Its Strategies and Tactics.* New York: Houghton Mifflin Co., 1913.

King, Josias R. "The Battle of Bull Run, A Confederate Victory Obtained but not Achieved." (MOLLUS, Minnesota). Minneapolis: Aug. Davis, 1909.

Lewis, Richard. *Camp Life of a Confederate Boy, Of Bratton's Brigade, Longstreet's Corps. C.S.A.* Charleston: News and Courier Book Presses, 1883.

Livermore, Thomas L. *Numbers and Losses in the Civil War in America 1861–1865.* Boston: Houghton Mifflin, 1902.

Lochren, William. "Narrative of the First Regiment." *Minnesota in the Civil War and Indian Wars 1861–1865.* Vol. I. St. Paul: Pioneer Press Co., 1891.

McAfee, Michael J. *Zouaves: The First and the Bravest.* Gettysburg: Thomas Publications, 1991.

McAllister, J. Gray. *Sketch of Captain Thompson McAllister, Citizen, Soldier, Christian.* Petersburg: Fenn and Owen, 1896.

Meagher, Thomas F. *The Last Days of the 69th in Virginia.* New York, 1861.

Merritt, John G. "A Minnesota Boy's First Battle." *Sabre and Bayonet: Stories of Heroism and Military Adventure.* Theo. F. Rodenbough, ed. New York: G.W. Dillingham Co., 1897.

Metcalf, Lewis H. "So Eager Were We All..." *American Heritage.* Vol. XVI, Number 4, June 1965.

Miller, Francis T. *The Photographic History of The Civil War.* 10 vols. New York: The Review of Reviews Co., 1912.

Moe, Richard. *The Last Full Measure: The Life and Death of the First Minnesota Volunteers.* New York: Henry Holt and Co., 1993.

Moore, Frank ed. *The Rebellion Record: A Diary of American Events.* 10 vols. New York: G.P. Putnam, 1861.

Mundy, James H. *Second to None: The Story of the 2nd Maine Volunteers "The Bangor Regiment."* Scarborough, Maine: Harp Publications, 1992.

Opie, John N. *A Rebel Cavalryman With Lee, Stuart and Jackson.* Chicago: W.B. Conkey Co., 1899.

Otis, George A. and D.L. Huntington. *The Medical and Surgical History of the War of the Rebellion.* Part 3, Vol. II. Washington: Government Printing Office, 1883.

Otis, George H. *The Second Wisconsin Infantry.* Alan Gaff, ed. Dayton: Morningside, 1984.

Our Firemen. Chapter XLII, "Fire Zouaves." U.S. Military History Institute, Archives Division, Carlisle, Pennsylvania.

Our Living and Our Dead: Devoted to North Carolina—Her Past, Her Present and Her Future. Vol. I. Raleigh: Southern Historical Society, 1874.

Peters, Winfield. "First Battle of Manassas." *Southern Historical Society Papers.* Vol. 34, 1906.

Robertson, Dr. James I. *The 4th Virginia Infantry.* Lynchburg: H.E. Howard, 1982.

———. *The Stonewall Brigade.* Baton Rouge: Louisiana State University Press, 1963.

Robinson, Frank T. *History of the Fifth Regiment, M.V.M.* Boston: W.F. Brown and Co., 1879.

Roe, Alfred S. *The Fifth Regiment Massachusetts Volunteer Infantry.* Boston: Fifth Regiment Veteran Association, 1911.

Sherman, William T. *Memoirs of General William T. Sherman.* New York: Da Capo Press, 1984.

Todd, William. *The Seventy-Ninth Highlanders.* Albany: Brandow, Barton and Co., 1886.

U.S. Congress. *Report of the Joint Committee on the Conduct of the War, In Three Parts: Bull Run to Ball's Bluff.* Part II. Washington, D.C.: Government Printing Office, 1863.

Wallace, Lee, Jr. *5th Virginia Infantry.* Lynchburg, Virginia: H.E. Howard, 1988.

Wallace, Robert C. *A Few Memories of a Long Life.* John M. Carroll, ed. Fairfield, Washington: Ye Galleon Press, 1988.

The War of the Rebellion: A Compilation of the Official Records of the Union and Confederate Armies. Ser. I. Vol. II and Vol. LI, pt. I. Washington, D.C.: Government Printing Office, 1880–1901.

Index

References to photographs are in italics.
First names are listed where known.

76